Clean Beaches

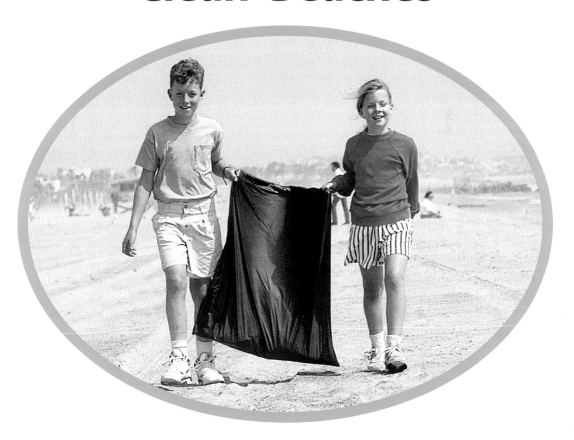

by Margie Burton, Cathy French, and Tammy Jones

I like to go to the beach.

We like to
go swimming.

I like to ride on a boat.

We like to eat at the beach.

But we don't like to see trash on the beach.

Trash is not good for the seals.
They can get trapped in it.

Trash is not good for the fish.
They can get trapped in it.

Trash is not good for the birds.
They can get trapped in it, too.

Trash is not good for the whales.
They eat it and it can make
them sick.

Trash is not good for the dolphins.
It can make them sick, too.

My friends and I do not like trash!
We are going to pick up all
the trash on the beach.

Big beach cleanups are held
in our country every September.

We will make the beach
look nice again.

We will put on gloves.

We will put the trash in bags.

We will pick up cups.

We will pick up cans.

Beach Trash

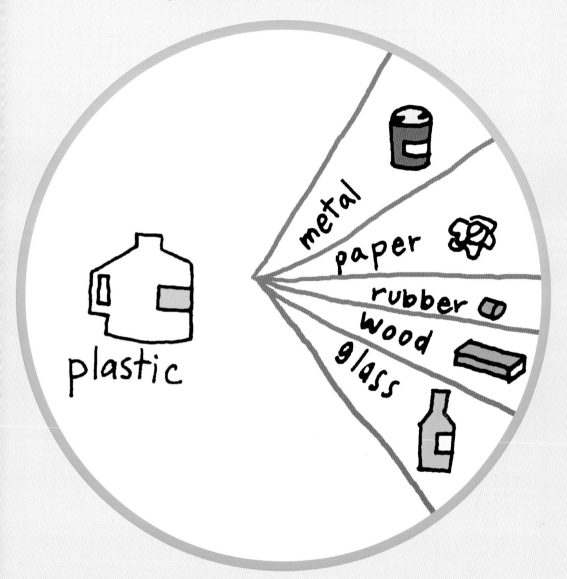

Most of the beach trash is made of plastic.
Can you see what the other trash is made of?

The Dirty Dozen

1		cigarettes
2		plastic pieces
3		foamed plastic pieces
4		plastic food bags/wrappers
5		plastic lids/caps
6		paper pieces
7		glass pieces
8		plastic straws
9		metal beverage cans
10		glass beverage bottles
11		plastic beverage bottles
12		plastic foam cups

The Dirty Dozen is the list of the twelve things that are found most often on United States beaches during the Coastal Cleanup.